WORLD of PLANTS

HOW PLANTS LIVE & GROW
for Young Scientists

WORLD of PLANTS

HOW PLANTS LIVE & GROW
for Young Scientists

Published by
Heron Books, Inc.
20950 SW Rock Creek Road
Sheridan, OR 97378

heronbooks.com

———————————

Special thanks to all the teachers and students who
provided feedback instrumental to this edition.

———————————

ISBN: 978-0-89-739243-3

Printed in the USA

13 May 2021

At Heron Books, we think learning should be engaging and fun. It should be hands-on and allow students to move at their own pace.

To facilitate this we have created a learning guide that will help any student progress through this book, chapter by chapter, with confidence and interest.

Get learning guides at
heronbooks.com/learningguides.

For teacher resources,
such as a final exam, email
teacherresources@heronbooks.com.

We would love to hear from you!
Email us at *feedback@heronbooks.com.*

Your YOUNG SCIENTIST JOURNAL

Scientists love to explore the world and how things in it work. They like to go new places and discover things they've never seen before.

They also like to keep track of what they find. They often fill books with notes and drawings of what they see, and include their thoughts and questions about it. These books are called *science journals.*

What's fun about a science journal is that you can use it to draw pictures or sketches of things that interest you. You can write down ideas you have about things, make maps, write down questions you have and things you want to find out more about. You might even stick in it samples of things you find—flowers, bugs, leaves, feathers, spider's webs—who knows what?

The learning guide that goes with this book will sometimes ask you to look at things and make notes or drawings in a journal of your own.

Whatever you put in your science journal, it will be full of your own personal discoveries. No two journals are alike.

You can use a journal like the one shown here, or you can use a notebook of your choice. You might even want to make your own science journal and use that.

Whichever type of journal you choose, it will be a place to keep drawings and notes about what you are finding out about the world and how it works.

So get ahold of a science journal, or make one, and then get going to see what you can find out. Who knows what might be waiting for you?

IN THIS BOOK

ONE WORLD
WORLD
THREE
KINGDOMS

There are so many, many things on our planet Earth. It's a wonderful and fascinating world.

Some of the most exciting things in our world were made by humans. From pyramids to french fries, from kites to surfboards, from firecrackers to rocket ships, people have been creating and making interesting and useful things for thousands of years.

But the world is full of many wonderful things not created by humans, things that are part of what we call the natural world.

This includes trees, rocks, rivers and mountains. It includes frogs, canyons, tigers and lightning. And there are fish, birds, flowers, bees, and miles and miles of deserts, oceans and fields of wild grass.

All of these natural things belong to three enormous groups that scientists call **kingdoms**.

THE ANIMAL KINGDOM

There is the **animal kingdom**, which includes all insects, birds, fish and mammals. It includes all the creatures of the sea and land. It includes animals like salamanders and crabs, storks and whales, cats and dogs.

Scientists have discovered that plants were here on Earth long before animals. They have also observed and named more than 250,000 different kinds of plants that live and grow in our world!

THE PLANT KINGDOM

Then there is the **plant kingdom**, which includes all the trees, bushes and grasses. It includes the plants that live in the ocean and the plants that grow in the highest mountains. It includes the mushrooms in the forest and kelp plants that can grow 250 feet tall under the ocean's surface.

THE MINERAL KINGDOM

The third group of natural things in the world is called the **mineral kingdom**. Unlike plants and animals, minerals are not alive. They include the rocks, sand and dirt of Earth. They include metals like gold and silver. The salt you use on your food is a mineral. There are many other minerals that plants and animals need to stay healthy.

You might think some things are minerals just because they aren't alive. But if they originally came from things that were alive, they aren't minerals.

For example, wood is not a mineral. It came from a tree. A piece of meat is not a mineral because it came from an animal.

And even though salt is a mineral, sugar is not. Salt comes from the ocean or from underground. Sugar comes from two different kinds of plants, sugar beets and sugar cane. So it is not a mineral.

Sometimes people enjoy arguing about whether certain things are part of the mineral kingdom. What about water or air? Hmmm. Interesting question. They certainly aren't plants or animals. But are they minerals?

Well, no, they are not actually minerals because minerals are solid. So rocks and metals like gold and silver are minerals. Scientists agree that air and water are not.

But whether you want to enjoy a good argument or not, it can help to know about these three kingdoms. With all the millions and millions of different natural things in the world, it's good to start with three simple groups.

One enormous world, but just three kingdoms. That's a good place to begin for any young scientist!

This book is about the world of plants, the plant kingdom.

SO, WHAT IS A PLANT?

We know that plants aren't animals, and they aren't minerals. But what exactly is a plant?

Like animals, plants are alive. They start small, they grow, they get old, and eventually they die.

In order to find food, animals have to move around. A bird might fly through the air to catch insects. A cat will hunt mice. Even cows have to keep moving to find more and more grass to eat.

But plants have a special ability. They can make their own food! How they do this is something we will learn about later in this book.

The fact that they don't have to move around to find food is the biggest difference between plants and animals.

Plants grow in the ground, in the water, or even on top of other plants!

Flower

Stem

Leaf

Plants are usually green, but some have other colors too. Sometimes a plant's red, blue or golden color will show up more strongly than its green color. Some plants are even grey or white.

Many plants can look very different from each other, but almost all plants have the same basic parts.

Look at any plants you can find nearby. You might not see the roots, but you should be able to see some of the parts. Look for the stem, the leaves and maybe flowers depending on the time of year.

You probably won't see the seeds of a plant just by looking at it. The seeds are usually inside the plant, often inside the plant's fruit. Can you think of a fruit that has seeds in it?

Whatever kind of plant it is, it will usually have these parts. And you won't find it chasing down its food because it makes its own. That's why it's a plant!

To grow, plants need water, air, sunlight and soil. **Soil** is the dirt that plants grow in.

When water, air, sunlight and soil are available in the right amounts, plants will live and grow. They will make flowers and seeds, and the seeds will then grow to make more plants.

Plants that grow in rainy areas use the most water, and plants that grow in deserts use the least. Plants that need warmth and lots of sun live in hot, sunny areas.

When plants grow without any help from people, we say they are growing **naturally**. They're getting good soil and enough sunlight and water where they are, without any help.

If you want to grow a plant that doesn't grow naturally in your area, then you have to make sure it gets the right amount of sunlight, water, air and soil. For example, if a plant comes from a place that is warm all year round, you may have to keep it indoors all year to keep it warm enough.

If you know what your plants need, and you give them the right amounts of those things, they will grow.

With a little practice, you can learn to grow lots of healthy, happy plants!

Let's Do This!

GROWING BEAN PLANTS

For this activity you will need

- a flower pot about 5 to 6 inches across with a hole in the bottom (You can also use a large plastic cup as long as you put a hole in the bottom.)

- a saucer big enough to hold the flower pot or cup

- potting soil

- 4 bean seeds (lima beans or kidney beans work well)

Steps

1 Fill the flower pot with potting soil up to just below the top of the pot.

2 The soil should be moist. If the soil is dry, pour a little water on top of the soil and let it soak in.

3 Poke several holes in the soil about 1 inch deep. Drop one seed in each hole and cover the holes with soil.

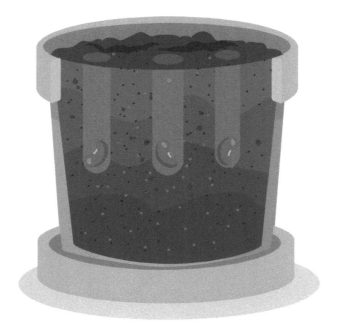

4 Put the pot in a place where it is okay for water to drip and drain away, such as a sink or tub. Gently pour water on the top of the soil until water comes out the bottom of the pot.

5 Let the pot drip. When it stops, put the pot on the saucer in a warm, sunny place so your bean seeds will be warm and have enough sunlight to sprout.

6 Check the pot each day to be sure the soil is moist. The seeds need to be moist all the time while they are starting to grow, or they will die. Each time you check, write the date and make a note in your science journal about what you can see.

After several days you should see some bean plants coming up.

If you keep giving them enough water and sunlight, they should grow to be healthy and beautiful.

Let's Do This!

WITH AND WITHOUT SUNLIGHT

For this activity you will need

- radish seeds
- 2 clear plastic cups of the same size
- potting soil
- measuring spoons
- plastic wrap
- 2 rubber bands
- masking tape

Steps

1. Put 2 tablespoons of soil in each cup.

2. Sprinkle about ¼ of a teaspoon of radish seeds on top of the soil and stir them in.

3. Add 1 teaspoon of water to each cup.

4. Cover each cup with plastic wrap and hold it in place with a rubber band. Poke holes in the plastic so the growing plants can get air.

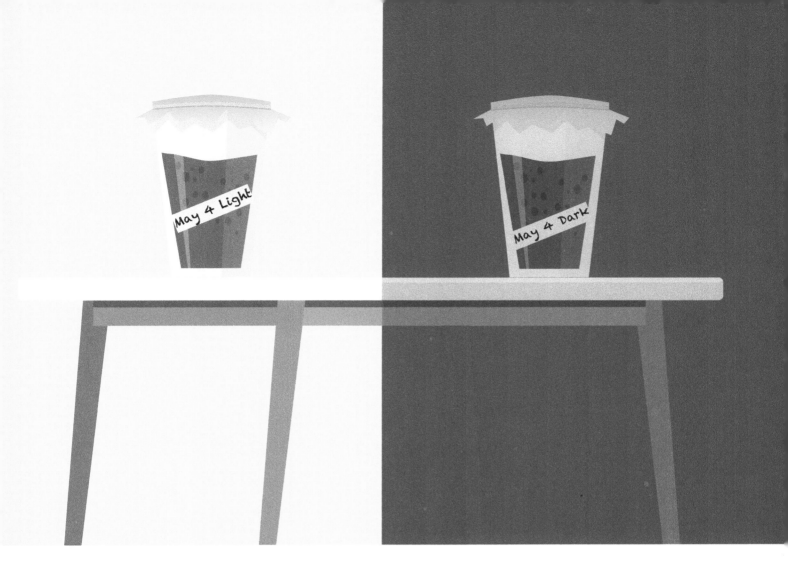

5. Write the date on two pieces of masking tape. Write "DARK" on one piece of tape and "LIGHT" on the other. Put one piece of tape on each cup.

6. Put the cup marked DARK in a dark place. Put the cup marked LIGHT in a place where it can get lots of light. Both places should be about the same temperature.

7. Check the cups every day. Each day, take notes or make sketches of your observations in your science journal.

8. Four or five days after the plants sprout, explain in your science journal what happened to the leaves and stems of the plants grown in the dark, and what happened to the plants grown in the light. Share what you wrote with your teacher.

4

People use plants in many ways. The most common way they are used is for food.

We know that plants make food for themselves but animals don't. Animals need to eat plants to get energy for living and growth, or they eat other animals that got their energy from eating plants. Without plants, animals would not be able to live on Earth.

The same is true for humans. We depend on plants for food.

Many plants are good to eat, as long as you eat the right part of the plant!

The good taste of vanilla ice cream comes from vanilla beans.

Bread is made from wheat.

The chocolate in chocolate bars comes from cocoa beans.

ROOTS

Roots are the parts of a plant that grow underground. Some plants have roots that make good food. These are called **root vegetables**.

carrot   beet   sweet potatoes   radish

STEMS

Some plants have stems that are good for eating. These are called **stem vegetables**.

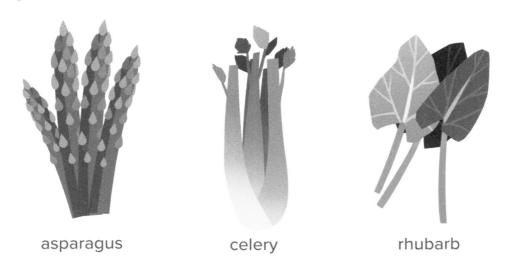

asparagus   celery   rhubarb

LEAVES

Did you know that people eat the leaves of some plants? These foods are leaf vegetables. People often call them **leafy greens**.

cabbage   lettuce   spinach   bok choy

FLOWERS

Have you ever eaten a flower? Maybe you did and didn't know it.

If you have ever eaten an artichoke, you've eaten a flower that was picked before it finished blossoming. If left to grow more, artichokes open up into beautiful pink, blue or violet flowers!

Some flowers are used to make tea. Rose tea is popular. Tea made from hibiscus flowers is also popular. It is sweet and bright red, like the petals of the hibiscus flower.

Here are a few examples of flowers people eat, even if they don't look like flowers when you eat them!

broccoli

artichoke

cauliflower

FRUITS

The fruit is the part of a plant you have probably eaten the most. Many fruits are healthy for you and often have a pleasant, sweet taste. Fruits have seeds inside them.

SEEDS

People eat many kinds of seeds. Some seeds, like sunflower seeds, are eaten by themselves. Other seeds, like wheat, are used to make things like bread and cereal.

Many beans are types of seeds. Lima beans are an example. Seeds of the cocoa plant are called cocoa beans. They are used to make chocolate.

As you can see, we find food from all the different parts of plants!

OTHER USES FOR PLANTS

5

WOOD

Another way people use plants is to make things, like paper, pencils, tables, chairs and houses. These are all made from wood that comes from trees.

Many different kinds of trees are used for their wood. Here are some of the most common ones.

oak

pine

maple

birch

COTTON

The cotton plant is used to make clothing.

The seeds of the cotton plant are surrounded by a fluffy material that looks like white cotton candy. This material is turned into thread and then woven into fabric. This fabric is used to make all kinds of things, from clothes and towels to tents and fishing nets.

DECORATION

Maybe you have some plants in your house. If so, they may be there for decoration.

Plants can be beautiful, especially when they are in attractive pots or planters.

If you want to make a room or yard more beautiful, one of the best ways to do it is by growing some plants.

ROOTS

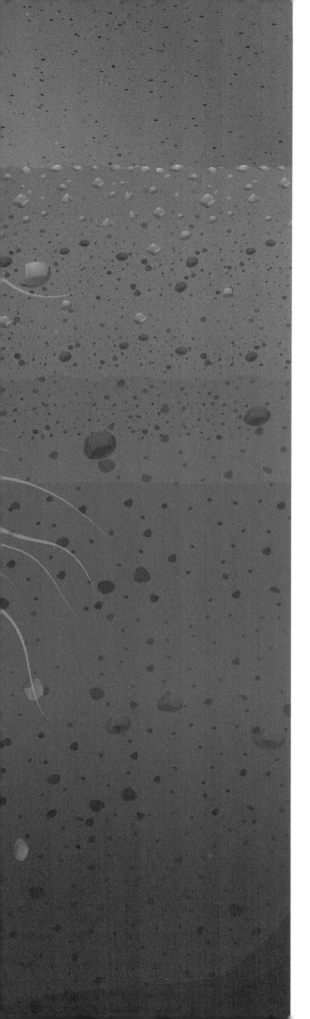

6

The roots of plants have a few different jobs.
One is to hold the plant in place.

Some plants have very long roots that go deep into the ground. Have you ever tried to pull up a very large weed? It's hard to do because the roots are so deep in the ground.

Tomato plants can have roots two feet long. The roots of some kinds of grass go almost six feet deep! Other plants have much shorter roots. Lettuce and cabbage have roots only one foot long, and onion roots are even shorter.

DRINKING

Water is very important to plants because it is one of the main things they are made of. You can see this for yourself by squashing a green leaf and feeling how wet it is inside. Plants must have water to grow.

Plants also need minerals, and they get them from the soil they're planted in.

So getting water and minerals from the soil is another important job that roots do. Water with minerals comes in through the roots and goes through tiny tubes to the rest of the plant.

The juicy apples on the highest branches of an apple tree are juicy because the roots are taking in water that gets sent all the way up to them!

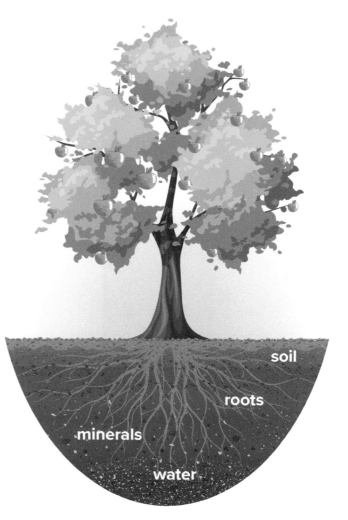

soil

roots

minerals

water

BREATHING

All plants need water, but most plants also need to have some air around their roots. When you grow plants in your house, you need to make sure they are getting enough water, but not too much.

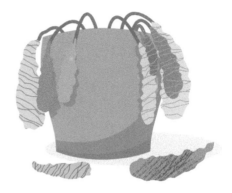

If your plant needs water, the soil will be dry. The leaves might also be **wilted**, which means they're hanging down, looking tired and unhappy.

Give your plant a drink and it should start to do better. Then remember to water it regularly.

Plants can't take too much water for very long. Plants that are in soil that is too wet can drown and die.

When soil has so much water that there is no air for the roots, we say it is **waterlogged.**

If your plant is waterlogged, the leaves may turn yellow and even fall off. Let the soil dry out for a few days and hopefully your plant will get better. Then try watering it less often.

Sometimes you have to get to know a plant well before you can be sure how much water it needs. Just keep a close eye on it and you will find out what makes it happy.

EXPLORING ROOTS

For this activity you will need

- an outside area where you can collect weeds

- tool for digging

- drawing materials

Steps

In this activity, you will be collecting some weeds so you can draw pictures of the plant and its roots.

1. Go outside and gently pull up a small weed. Get as much of the root out as you can.

2. Now find a weed that you can't pull up (or one that is very hard to pull up). Get some help if you need to, and pull it up or dig it out.

3. Bring both weeds in, and notice the differences between the roots of the two weeds.

4. Draw a picture of each plant and its roots in your science journal. Write down two important jobs that roots do. Share your work with your teacher.

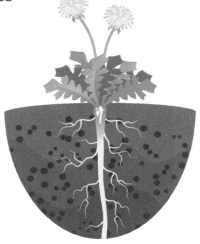

5. Show your drawing, and tell (or write up for) someone two important jobs roots do.

7

The **stem** of a plant, the main part that grows above the ground, holds up its other parts like the leaves and flowers.

TREES AND BUSHES

Most trees and bushes are woody. That means they have wood in their stems and branches. The wood in them makes their stems strong. This makes it possible for the plants to grow large.

Near the center of a tree or bush the stems are larger. Stems get smaller toward the edges. The smallest stems at the ends of branches are called **twigs**.

A **bush** is similar to a tree, but it's smaller and doesn't have a trunk. A bush has many smaller stems (also called branches) that grow right out of the ground instead of from a trunk.

On the other hand, most flowers, grasses and vegetable plants are green and soft. Their stems are not woody, so they are not able to grow as large.

VINES

Some plants have another kind of stem that is not quite woody and not quite soft and green.

Vines are plants that grow on long thin stems that are not strong enough to stand upright by themselves. A vine may grow along the ground like a pumpkin vine, or it may crawl up buildings and trees like ivy does.

Vine stems start off green and soft, but if they live more than one year, parts of the stem can turn to wood, making the vine much stronger.

A pumpkin vine lives only one year and remains green and soft, but an ivy vine lives for many years. If you look at old ivy vines growing on trees or buildings, you can see where parts of the stems have turned to wood.

HOW STEMS WORK

Minerals and water travel from the ground through the roots of a plant to the stems. Stems have tiny tubes running up through them that carry the water and minerals to the leaves.

It is the leaves that use minerals and water that have come up from the ground to make food for the rest of the plant. This food doesn't use the tubes that carry water and minerals. It travels through different tubes in the stem to the other parts of the plant.

The liquid traveling through both tubes in the stems of a plant is called **sap**.

Some insects and birds feed on plant sap. And if you've ever had maple syrup on pancakes, you eat sap too. Maple syrup is the sap from a sugar maple tree.

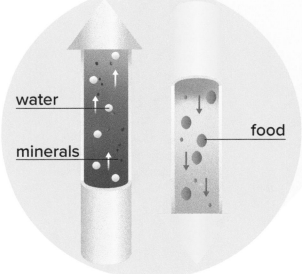

water

minerals

food

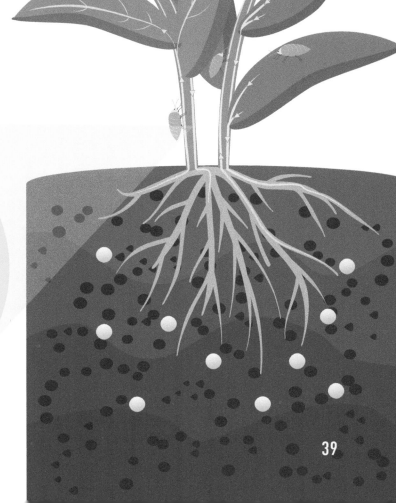

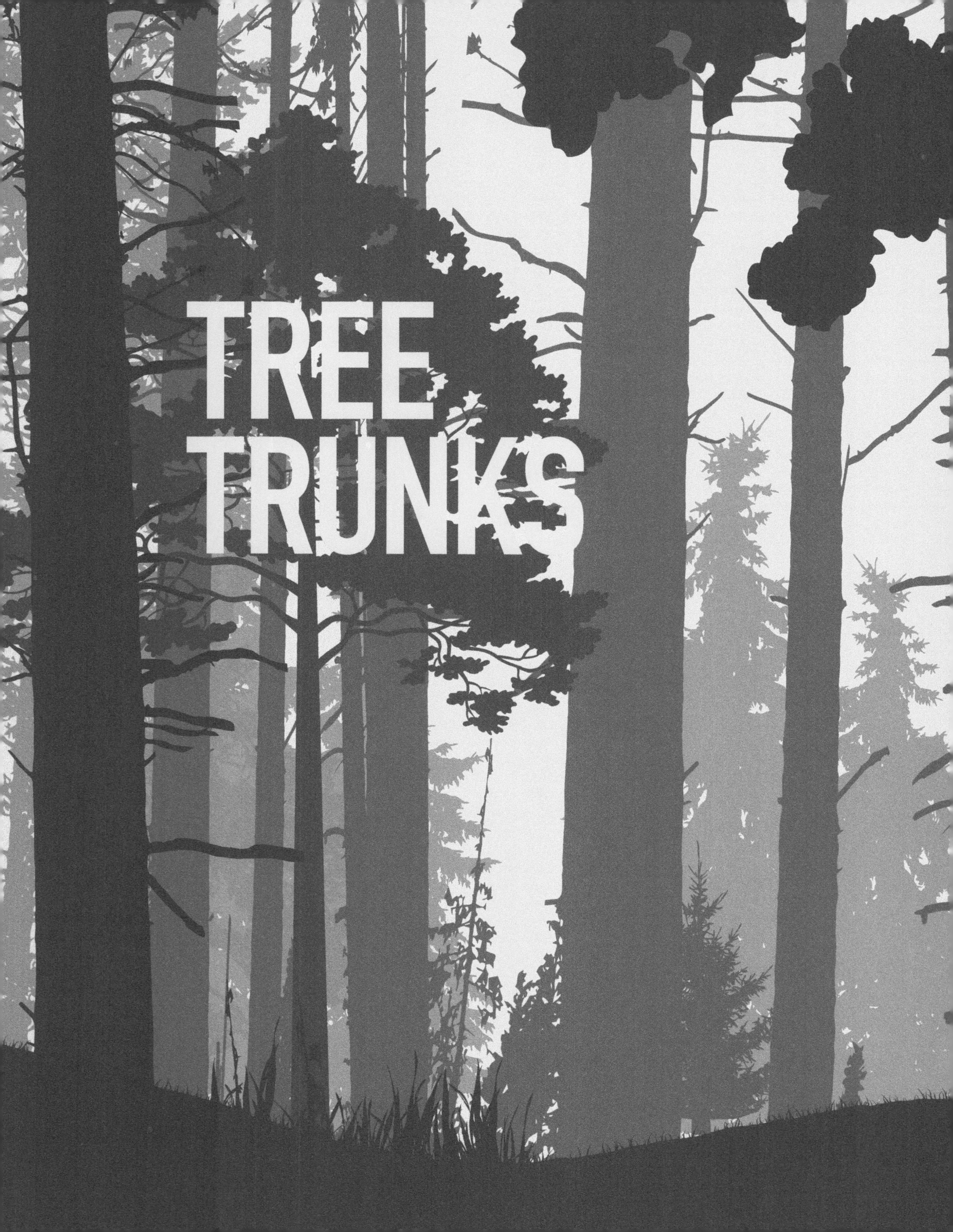
TREE
TRUNKS

8

Trees can live for many, many years. Because they live so long, their stems, or trunks, can become very large.

The largest tree in the world is a giant sequoia tree in California. It's so well-known, it has a name. It's called the General Sherman Tree after a famous army commander. Scientists think this tree is over 2,000 years old.

The trunk and branches of a tree are all part of its stem. As with all stems, the trunk of a tree carries water and minerals from the roots to the leaves, and food from the leaves to the rest of the tree.

The trunk and branches of a tree are full of tiny tubes that are so small you can barely see them. If you were to cut the trunk or a branch straight across and look at it with a microscope, there they would be!

Let's look more closely at the parts of a tree trunk, starting with the outside. Here is an illustration that shows what you would find.

BARK

The outside part of a tree trunk or branch is called the **bark**. The bark is made of two parts, the outer bark and the inner bark

1 The outer bark keeps the tree from drying out and protects it from animals and bad weather.

2 The inner bark contains the little tubes that carry the sap from the leaves *down* to the roots and other parts of the tree. This inner bark does not carry the sap that goes up from the roots. That job is done in another part.

CAMBIUM

③ The next layer inside a tree trunk and branches is very thin. It's called the **cambium** (KAM bee um). This is where the tree grows a little thicker every year. It adds some inner bark to its outside and it also adds a little bit to the cambium.

SAPWOOD

④ Moving further toward the center of the trunk and branches, we have the layers where little tubes carry water and minerals *up* from the soil. These layers are called **sapwood**. In a living tree the sapwood is usually light in color and wet. You can see the lighter color in the picture.

Even though the liquid in a tree is called sap when it is going both *down* from the leaves and *up* from the roots, only these layers carrying sap *up* are called sapwood.

HEARTWOOD

⑤ The wood in the very center of a trunk or a branch is called **heartwood**. This is usually darker than the sapwood. It is the oldest part of the tree, and in an old tree there is more heartwood than sapwood.

As sapwood gets older it turns into heartwood. The tubes in the inner part of the sapwood gradually get clogged up and stop carrying water and minerals, and so it becomes heartwood.

Heartwood gives a tree strength, but it no longer carries sap.

TREE RINGS

Each spring the cambium inside a tree grows, forming new sapwood and new inner bark. The tree grows bigger. In the fall the cambium stops growing until spring.

Each year the new growth forms a whole ring of new wood inside the trunk.

When a tree is cut down, you can see the inside of the trunk, including these rings, which we call **tree rings**. You can count how many years old a tree is by the number of rings it has.

Looking at tree rings you can also tell when a tree grew more and when it grew less. If two rings are far apart, the tree grew a lot that year. If they are close together, the tree did not grow much that year. This can be caused by not enough rain or unusual weather that year.

Scientists don't have to cut a tree down to tell how old it is. They have a way to remove a small section of the trunk with a special tool. They look at this section to count the rings.

Most trees have tree rings, but not all. Some, like palm trees for example, grow differently inside the stem and don't have clear growth rings.

SOME VERY OLD TREES

Many trees can live to be over 100 years old. A few, like the General Sherman Tree, can live for several thousands of years. Here are a few of the oldest trees in the world that scientists have discovered and given special names to.

Scientists believe Methuselah (muh THOO zuh luh) is 4,850 years old. This tree is named after a man who, according to legend, lived almost a thousand years. It lives in an area of the White Mountains in California. The exact location is kept secret for the safety of the tree.

Old Tjikko (CHEE koh) is a spruce tree that lives in the mountains of Sweden, in northern Europe. Old Tjikko is believed to be almost 10,000 years old, but is a little different from the other trees talked about here. About every 600 years, it sprouts a new trunk from its original roots, which are about 9,500 years old. This trunk grows into a new tree, but one with ancient roots.

In Spanish, Gran Abuelo (ah BWAY loh) means "great grandfather." This is a good name for a tree that is 3,646 years old. It is the oldest living tree in South America. Its home is the country of Chile. Gran Abuelo is 200 feet tall and 36 feet across!

If you ever get a chance to visit a park that has very old trees, you can go meet one yourself. There may even be trees that are hundreds of years old near where you live!

SOFTWOOD AND HARDWOOD

9

TWO KINDS OF TREES

Some trees have harder wood than other trees. They are harder to cut or carve into shapes. We call this kind of tree a **hardwood tree** and its wood is called **hardwood**.

We call trees with softer wood **softwood trees** and their wood is called **softwood**.

We get most softwood from trees that stay green all year long and don't lose their leaves or needles. These are called **evergreen trees**, because they are always green.

Most evergreen trees have needles for leaves and cones instead of fruit or nuts. Some evergreens are used as Christmas trees because they are still green and beautiful in winter.

We get most hardwood from trees that lose their leaves once a year and then grow them back the next. Trees like this are called deciduous (di SIJ oo us). **Deciduous** means the leaves fall off every year.

Deciduous trees are often very beautiful in the fall, especially when many different kinds are growing near each other.

Not all softwood is that soft, and not all hardwood is that hard. Here's a test you can make for hardness.

Take a piece of wood and press down on it with your fingernail. If your fingernail goes into the wood a little bit and makes a small dent, it's a pretty soft wood. If you can't easily make a dent in the wood, it's a fairly hard wood.

USES OF SOFTWOOD AND HARDWOOD

Softwood is easier to use in woodworking. For example, if you wanted to make a birdhouse, a wooden rocket, or a bookshelf, you might want to choose a type of softwood.

Softwood is also better for carving small wooden sculptures.

Lumber mills, where logs are cut into different shapes of wood, often use softwood to make lumber for building houses. Paper is also made from softwood.

Sometimes you want to use hardwood so that the things you build are stronger and tougher and will last longer. For this reason, hardwoods are often used to make furniture, floors and wood decorations, such as wood statues and picture frames.

Another good thing about hardwoods is that many of them, oak and maple for example, are quite attractive so they make handsome furniture, cabinets and floors.

When you look outside, do you see some trees?

Do they have leaves that fall off in the winter? If so, they are deciduous trees, and the wood they give us is hardwood.

Do you see trees with needles that stay green all year? Those are evergreen trees, and their wood is softwood.

You can find many different kinds of hardwood and softwood trees living in North America today!

LEAVES

10

A **leaf** is a flat part of a plant that grows out of the stem. In a few plants, leaves grow out of the roots.

Leaves are usually green. Sometimes, however, they can be red, brown, yellow, white or even black!

On many deciduous trees, the leaves are green through spring and summer. Then they turn yellow, orange or red before falling off in autumn. On some trees, the leaves turn yellow, then orange, then red.

Blade

Most leaves have two main parts. The first part is the wide flat part. This is called the **blade**.

Leaf stalk

The second part is the thin piece that connects the leaf to the stem or root. This is the **leaf stalk**.

Some leaves don't have a leaf stalk. Instead they are attached directly to a stem or root.

The leaves of some plants don't look like normal leaves. They may be long and narrow like the needles of an evergreen tree. Or they might even look a little like the scales of a fish! Leaves like this don't have leaf stalks either.

One of the wonderful things about leaves is that they can have so many different shapes. When you get to know more about different kinds of plants, one way you can tell what plant it is, is by looking at its leaves.

Leaves take in light and warmth from the sun.

Leaves receive water and minerals that come from roots.

LEAF MAGIC

Of all the parts of a plant, leaves have one of the most important jobs. They feed the plant. They make its food!

This special ability of leaves is one of the things that makes plants different from animals. It's what makes plants so valuable. If you recall, animals cannot make their own food. To get the food they need to live and grow, animals must eat plants or other animals that eat plants.

Carbon dioxide

Leaves take in carbon dioxide. **Carbon dioxide** (KAR bun dye AHK side) is part of the air around us. It gets added to our air when people and animals breathe out, and when things are burned. Too much carbon dioxide is not healthy for people to breathe in, so it's very helpful that the leaves of plants remove it from the air we breathe.

The carbon dioxide enters a leaf through tiny holes in its surface. These holes are so small you need a microscope to see them.

Leaves magically use carbon dioxide, water, minerals and sunlight to make food for the plant.

The leaves feed the plants so the plants can make more roots, stems and leaves. They also use the food to make flowers.

And because leaves do their magic so well, animals and humans have a way to get the energy they need to live and grow. If leaves didn't do their magic, we would not be able to live and grow ourselves!

Let's Do This!

CREATING A LEAF DISPLAY

For this activity you will need

- Several sheets of plain paper

- 3 or 4 large books

- Cardboard or heavy poster board

- Glue

- Pen or marker

Steps

1. Collect leaves from five or more plants that you like.

2. Lay your leaves on a sheet of plain paper. Make sure the leaves don't touch each other. You may need more than one sheet of paper.

3. Next to each leaf, write the name of the plant it came from. If you don't know the name, find out what it is.

4. Put another sheet of paper on top of your leaves.

5. Put the leaves and paper under a stack of three or four heavy books. This will flatten the leaves and dry them out.

6. After four or five days, glue your leaves to the cardboard or poster board in a nice display. Next to each leaf, write the name of the plant it came from and any other information you want to put about it.

FLOWERS

11

So far, we've learned about the parts of a plant that help it live and grow.

Its roots drink up water and minerals from the soil. Its stems carry these to the leaves. Its leaves do their food-making magic. And its stems carry that food from the leaves to all parts of the plant.

Now, let's talk about the flowers of a plant, which have a very different job. They don't actually help the plant live and grow.

Instead, their job is to help make more plants! And the way they do this is one of the most fascinating things about plants.

Let's see how it happens.

PARTS OF A FLOWER

Flowers come in many different shapes and colors, but they all have the same parts. And all flowers do the same job.

Petals

Petals are the brightly colored parts grouped together around the center of a flower. Petals can be found in all different colors, including white. Often they smell good. The bright colors and attractive smell help bring insects to the plant. (You will find out later why this is important.)

Pistil

When a flower opens and the petals spread out, you can see the middle part of the flower. This is called the **pistil** (PIS tul). Pistils can have many different shapes.

Seeds

No matter what it looks like, the pistil is always in the center of the flower. And it has a very important job. This is where the seeds of the plant are made, the seeds that will someday become new plants of the same kind!

Stamens

There are small thread-like arms sticking up around the pistil. These are called **stamens** (STAY muhnz). Flower stamens produce a powder you may have heard of called **pollen** (POL un). A flower uses pollen to make seeds. And this is where things gets interesting.

Pollen

For a seed to be created, pollen has to somehow travel from the tips of the stamens to the pistil. When it does, it combines with something inside the pistil and one or more seeds begin to grow. Transferring pollen from the stamens of a flower to the pistil is called **pollination** (pol uh NAY shun) and it is how plants make seeds.

Sepal

The green leafy part just below the flower's petals is called the **sepal** (SEE pul).

Bud

Before a flower has opened up, or bloomed, it is fully or partly covered by its sepal. This protects the inside parts from weather and insects. A flower that hasn't yet opened up and is still covered by the sepal is called a **bud**.

Have you ever watched a bee going from flower to flower on the same plant? The bee is moving pollen from the stamens of one flower to the pistil of another flower on that plant.

Many flowers attract birds, bees, butterflies, moths and other insects to help move the pollen. Their bright colors and sweet smells tell insects to come get a taste of a sweet, sticky juice the flower makes called **nectar** (NEK tur).

POLLINATION

So remember, to create seeds, pollen has to get from the stamens to the pistil. How does this happen?

There are two main ways that pollination happens.

Here's one. Insects or birds come to a flower, they touch the stamens and some of its pollen sticks to them. If they then touch the pistil, some of the pollen rubs off onto that. And presto, they've transferred pollen from the stamens to the pistil!

Some insects and birds like to eat pollen. When they see or smell a flower that has opened up, they know there's some good food waiting for them.

Whether it comes for nectar or pollen, when an insect moves around on a flower, it brushes up against the stamens. The pollen dust from the stamens sticks to its body. If the insect then flies to another flower and moves around on that, the pollen from the original flower is spread to the new flower.

Another way pollination happens is with the help of the wind. The pollen of some plants is easily blown into the air. The wind carries it to another plant, where it lands on the pistil. A lot of grasses pollinate this way.

The way wind-pollinated plants make sure of successful pollination is to make huge amounts of pollen. Perhaps in the spring you've seen lots of yellowish dust settle outdoors on things like sidewalks or cars. This is pollen from evergreen trees, grasses and other plants that use the wind to pollinate. On a field of grass you might even see what looks like a cloud of dust blowing across it. This is actually a cloud of grass pollen!

Some people have a bad reaction when this happens. It makes them sneeze and their eyes get itchy and red. When this happens, they might try to stay indoors until there is less pollen in the air.

THE END OF THE FLOWER

Most flowers bloom in the spring. This is when you see bees humming from plant to plant, and birds excited about building or finding nests in which to lay their eggs to start a new family.

A few weeks after they bloom, flowers begin to die. The petals fade in color. Then they crumple up and fall off.

But in the meantime, pollination has made it possible for seeds to start forming inside the pistil! As the petals die, so does the top of the pistil. But in the bottom of the pistil, seeds are starting to grow.

Most flowers produce many seeds. So this is the beginning of many new plants. The beautiful, fascinating flower has done its job!

SEEDS

12

So, after a flower dies, what happens to the seeds that have started growing in the pistil?

Let's find out!

A plant seed grows inside a shell or **seed coat** that protects the seed and contains enough food for the seed to start growing.

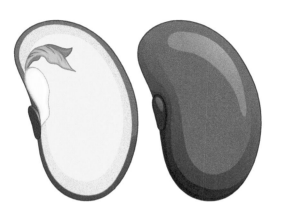

Sometimes seeds are formed in groups. The peas in a peapod are a good example of this.

Seeds come in every size and shape. The seed of the huge redwood tree is only the size of the period at the end of this sentence.

The seed of a coconut tree is quite large. How large? As large as a coconut, because a coconut is the seed of a coconut tree!

Fruits are a little different. In many fruits, the bottom part of the pistil gets bigger and bigger as the seeds inside it grow. It finally becomes the fruit that we like to eat. Apples, pears and tomatoes are examples of this.

In some kinds of plants, a shell or pod forms with the seeds inside it. When the shell or pod splits open, the seeds come loose. Many nuts are examples of this.

Seeds in fruit eaten by an animal can be carried a long distance and dropped to the ground as part of the animal's waste.

Some seeds have silky hairs that allow the seed to be lifted and carried off by the wind.

HOW SEEDS ARE SPREAD

Plants usually make many more seeds than are needed to grow new plants. That way, even if most of the seeds are eaten or die, some will still grow into new plants.

To grow, seeds need soil, water and light, and enough room to grow into a plant. Sometimes they just fall to the ground and find exactly what they need. Sometimes they are carried to new places, by the wind, for example.

Many years ago, there were no apple trees in all of North America. Then people coming to America from Europe brought apple seeds with them. They planted these around their new homes, and before long many American villages and farms had lots of apple trees. Now you can find apple trees growing in every single state in the U.S.

TIME TO GROW UP

A seed has in it everything a new plant needs to start growing. It has its tough seed coat to protect it. And it has food inside the seed coat it can use for growing.

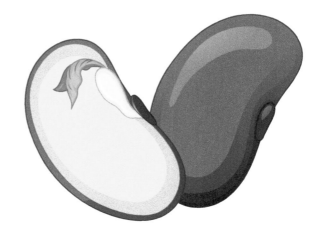

Most important, the seed has a tiny new plant in it. This new plant is called the **embryo** (EM bree oh).

The embryo may not look like a plant when it is still inside the seed, but it will soon after it starts growing.

A seed will last a long time without growing as long as it doesn't get wet.

Some seeds need to go through a cold season before they will start to grow. But most will start growing as soon as they get water and are warm enough.

When a seed starts growing into a plant, the embryo turns into a **sprout** or a **seedling**. When this happens, we say the plant is **sprouting**.

Until a sprout has grown several roots and leaves, it continues getting its food from the seed. Once it has used up all the food in the seed, it's ready to start making its own food like a grown-up plant. It starts using its roots to get water and minerals, and it gets light from the sun and carbon dioxide from the air.

Once a seedling has grown roots and leaves, all that's left of the seed is a dried-up shell. The plant doesn't need this anymore. It's living on its own!

So, although there are some plants that don't start from seeds, most do. This means that almost every plant you see, whether it is indoors or outside, whether it is large or small, or young or old, most likely started out as a seed!

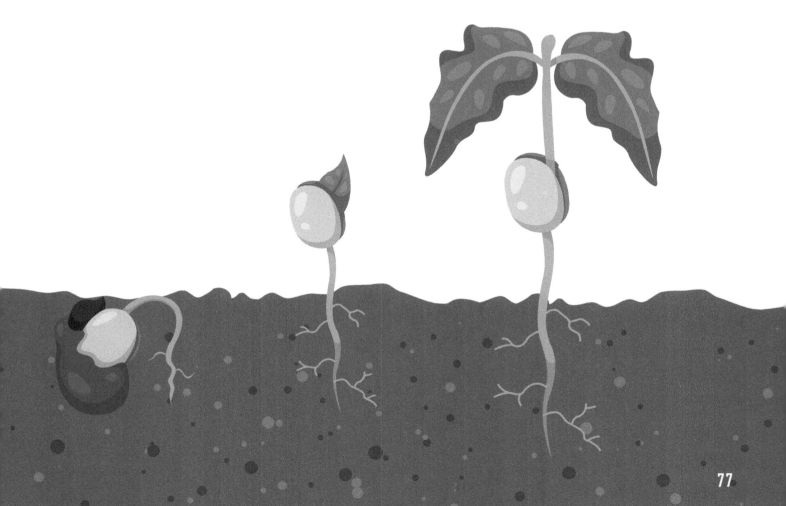

Let's Do This!

GROWING RADISH SPROUTS

For this activity you will need

- radish seeds

- a tall clear glass or jar

- measuring spoons

- a clean piece of pantyhose or cheesecloth

- a large rubber band

Steps

1. Put about ½ teaspoon of radish seeds into the glass or jar.

2. Cover the seeds with water.

3. Stretch the piece of pantyhose or cheesecloth across the top of the glass. Place the rubber band around the top to hold it in place.

4. Let the seeds soak overnight, then pour off the water.

5 Look at the sprouts in your jar once every day. In your science journal, write down the date and any difference you notice in the sprouts.

6 Afterward, rinse the sprouts. To do this, leave the covering on the jar. Pour fresh water through it into the jar. Swirl the water around, then pour it out. If any seeds stick to the covering, tap it so they fall back down to the bottom of the jar.

7 In a few days, you should have radish sprouts. Rinse the sprouts one more time, then drain the water. Take the sprouts out of the jar. In your science journal, draw a picture of one. Taste them if you want to. You can also put them on a sandwich or add them to a salad!

SOME STRANGE AND UNUSUAL PLANTS

13

A plant is an amazing form of life. From the magic of its leaves and the beauty of its flowers to all the tasty fruits and vegetables plants make, it's hard to imagine life without the plants that are all around us.

Let's finish exploring the wonderful world of plants by talking about a few plants that are particularly interesting.

VENUS FLYTRAP

Most plants use water and minerals from the soil, along with sunlight to make all the food they need. But there are plants that get their food in a very different way.

They eat bugs!

A famous insect-eating plant is the Venus flytrap.

This plant lives mainly on the east coast of the United States. It has tiny hairs inside a little trap that grows at the end of each of its leaves. When an insect or spider walks onto the surface of the open trap, the plant feels it with its tiny hairs and suddenly slams shut! Breakfast is caught!

The main diet of a Venus flytrap is ants, spiders, beetles and grasshoppers.

After about ten days of digesting its food, the trap opens back up, ready for more.

PITCHER PLANT

The Venus flytrap is not the only plant that eats insects. The pitcher plant is another. But it has a totally different method.

A pitcher plant traps insects inside hollow leaves filled with liquid it makes.

When an insect gets too far into the leaf, they can't climb back up again. They slip to the bottom, drown and are digested by the plant.

A type of pitcher plant that lives in the Philippines can grow to be five feet tall. This plant can even catch and digest small animals like lizards and mice!

BAOBAB TREE

There is a very unusual tree that grows in many African countries. It is called the baobab (BAY oh bab) tree.

In Africa, this amazing tree is called "the tree of life." Baobab trees not only become enormous, but they live for thousands of years.

After the first thousand years or so, they start to become hollow on the inside. They can then be used for storing things, or even for living inside.

Baobab trees can grow to be nearly 100 feet tall and some get to be just as big around!

The baobab is like a cactus because it can store water inside it. During Africa's rainy season it stores a lot of water in its trunk. This water helps it live through the long period of very hot, dry weather that follows.

The baobab is unusual in another way. During the hot dry season, when food can become scarce, the water it has stored helps it produce large fruit people can eat.

This is a good reason to think of it as the tree of life!

Baobab trees are helpful in so many ways that in hot, dry Africa many people choose to live near one of these wonderful trees.

These are just a few of the many amazing
and unusual plants that exist on Earth.

What else is there to learn about our
wonderful world of plants?

You're a young scientist.
Go find out!

Printed in the USA
CPSIA information can be obtained
at www.ICGtesting.com
JSHW072319020224
56506JS00020B/55